IMPOSSIBLE BUILDINGS

IMPOSSIBLE BUILDINGS

Poems by
Judith Johnson Sherwin

1973
Doubleday & Company, Inc., Garden City, New York

4/1973
Genl.

ISBN: 0-385-01859-2 Trade
0-385-01862-2 Paperbound

Library of Congress Catalog Card Number 72–94759

CONTENTS

6

8

IMPOSSIBLE BUILDINGS

ONE

VINEGAR TO DRINK

Look, now they come, the channering rains come down,
The years, the rains, with worrying tongue and tone;
Water rubs steel to rust and rain rots bone,
Rots hands, rots brows worn down with their long frown.
Living and dead, flesh melts and teeth stain brown,
The firm brain turns, like butter on warm stone,
Runny and brown again, and down they drone:
The churning, channering rains still chisel down.

Look, now the round clouds close, and now they wean
Their rust-robed crying Child, their grief-stained green
Worn Knight of bitter drink and crown of thorn—
They chide no more; the years, the tears, the lean
Embittered rains find Him eroded clean:
The eaten Bone then feels no need to mourn.

EURYDICE: TO ORPHEUS

Hear them, the songs, the sharp sparks of the lyre,
High, the harsh burning chords, the hard light,
Blue flames running on wires, a net, a barbed sky,
A rage, a hunger to tame or free the beast: which?
You will wake, you will mourn when I tell you,
When you hear it, the absence.
They are clear gone out, they are clean devoured,
Quenched now and quelled, the rites of your mystery.
We lived on blue flames once.
They are clean gone out, the bones of the voyager;
Old Argo sleeps in the blue sea, made soft with water,
And the waves sally and shun, and ever and again
Blue tongues wake in the wreck
And the waters move.
You lie in that blue sheet,
Burning, the shining life there shuddering your bones;
Water builds you anew, the sea dresses you
In a fitful revival.
I know no way out of death; we are here.

Silence, giver of life, renewer, deep water lapping
Salt and taste of blood,
Build me my life again out of this paralysis
Soft and phosphorescent in the flames.
I see your lips pale in the shivering light
Which breaks where it caresses
And your hands quiver with work of the shifty sea
And your forehead bleeds again;
A flower blooms red upon your face,
Torn, shredded by the bacchante's tooth and claw
And silence swells upon your clear voice.

THE GRASSES

spotted by gold and black of low-slung clouds
they rippled and rocked the field of their skin / while underneath
at the root of each hair burrowed, busy, a crowd
of parasites. restless, they stretched their claws out: great beast

testing, felt sun fleck the hide / shade / spots
shudder upon the skin. supine, the creature lay
muscles tensing to know what kills and rots,
body shrinking, chilled, crouched, tightened to meet the shade.

the wind that chilled them welded them into one,
threaded their nerves to a single sense swayed equally
by such a unity as no far sun
flickering, fickle, uneven in passion, could make them feel.

only with night they knew the enemy;
together in dread they bent to their greyed, unrested nerves
and from the borders of wood and brush saw singly
file / clicking their claws tiger and pard and carrion bird;

saw woman-headed lion and bull-faced man,
hippogriff slashing with steel-bladed wings and snorting flame,
coiling his scaly throat; saw silently how ran
there, neck and neck in their heat, the tireless werewolf and his mate;

saw; waited in animal terror to endure
humor and bruise of death; drew in their flexible / smooth
fibres; and felt, savage, the herd of sure
exultant centaurs shake their fierce and delicate trampling hooves.

tonight and all night, all nights, they, shrinking, meet
those careless, powerful wastrels, vulture, harpy and gull:
the hungry world let loose in its elegance and fleet
to gallop with graceful heads / devouring as they run.

THE BALANCE

darling here's my head
on a platter I promised you. if
you don't care for it that
much it doesn't matter. you can see the head
I trust, mine all right, but it's been
polished, a high shine put
onto the temples. to do that I had to take
everything wet off, sorry, or spill it out.

if you'd rather
I can give you my heart as usual it's all
wet (you can keep the platter) I have
a sieve at hand for the heart and though the head
is dead the heart can live
a while in the sieve it can turn around it can puff
in and out in and out like a frog's sides, fret, it can rub
a fine stinging rain through the fine cutting mesh
of the sieve it can fall on you
and wet you through.

you're the one has to weigh
please a merry measure
whether for one more time now
with that clear sterile skull to take
your pleasure or that soft pulsing slime.

DOMINE DEUS

the Lamb, that dies and lives in God still, praises
Hunger, that shall dispense flesh for the asking.

the Lion, reading deep in bloodshed, praises
Time, that shall make a killing of his killings.

the Child, in pause before his crying, praises
Joy, that shall sign in blood his ripe dominion.

the Man, in power of his senses, praises
Pain, that shall bear a hair-shirt for his loving.

the God, in radiance of his vigor, praises
Weakness, that shall give deeds for every blessing.

the Poet, whose high need is praising, praises
All, that shall put one limit to his praising.

GARDEN

in the place where shadows meet
i carved myself a cold retreat:
tall in pillars, dumb in stone
the gods grew, each upon his throne
to watch with square-cut alien eyes
the chiseled trees and foliage rise,
roses burst in bloom of rock,
lilies spring their marble lock,
quartz-grained petals fountain up
and fall to fill a frozen cup,
in frozen need the creatures move
each in his proper icy groove,
and every savage natural act
comes measured and in touch exact;

watchful gods stand side by side:
so shadowed out, no thought can hide;
moments, single and alone,
come padding still on paws of stone,
dog-headed act and feline sense

crouch in a clearness of one tense
to spring in concentrated leaps
each beast complete, no heights, no deeps;

division has no place in time:
the ivy mind may rise and climb
unbroken in a looping coil
all trees that stand from its own soil,
and find each trunk a constant home
to syphon comfort from its loam;

i am become a moment too:
stone rosemary and crystal rue,
whatever instants Dis let go
with loosened fingers, here may grow;
so fallen for a time in grace
these hands transfuse clover and mace;
herbs, spices winging from the eyes,
wheat for the hair alive may rise
and pull the quickened body straight
to stand in stone before the gate;

nor let some touch of harsh and rough
crush down my leaves, my idols bow;
hold fast: i have not slept enough
to lie, waking, now.

"There have been lovers who thought love should be
So much compounded of high courtesy
That they would sigh and quote with learned looks
Precedents out of beautiful old books. . . ."

—Yeats

LOVE

Then quote the precedents:
   out of the fire heat
out of the atom strength
   to bend all force to peace
out of the empty dead
   a dish that worms may eat
out of the Fall the shed
   blood to wash down this meal
out of the world no less
   life left us than we see
no pain but to amend
   a lacklife in what we feel
no joy but brings an end
   of joy to you and me

out of our hunger skill
   to grind our bones to rest:
here at the center, sit
   down, say grace to death.

DESIRE TO BE FORGOTTEN

desire to be forgotten, think
that taste is least of what we drink,
all need impersonal, all ease
fierce, passing superfluities.
what you must lose I cannot keep
there is no well in me so deep.

or if I lie, tell me how long
coolness lingers on the tongue,
how soon, deserting nerve and thirst
the rivers rinse out and are lost.
all day your taste was on my mouth;
remember it in day of drought.

THE LIGHT WOMAN'S SONG

love me with the left hand
leave me with the right
love me at height of day
leave before night

let no scurrying pulse tell
sunken in the vein
what the rough hounds bell
when they give tongue

what cunning the fox gnaws
panting in covert
what every beast knows
hide from your heart

left-handed lovers know
what I cast to know
what shall I hunger for
and not let go

"To see our selves againe wee neede not looke for Platoes yeare; every man is not onely himselfe; there have been many Diogenes, and as many Timons, . . . men are lived over againe, the world is now as it was in ages past, there was none then, but there hath been some one since that parallels him, and is as it were his revived selfe."

—*Sir Thomas Browne*

PLATO'S YEAR

When my friend came to Ayoda the streets of that town were torn
With weeds and long roots; stone cracked, in ditches cement melted
Like blood from a cracked heart, spouting; the towers at his return
Spat down their teeth; all burst apart that had been bolted;
Foundations, slowly crushed together and drawn down under, collapsed,
Their pits filled with what they were made to hold out; the trees bore
Their weight of Winter no longer than I can tell it; what lapsed
Was not less than civilization, when he came in the great year.

> Sure, I remember Spring.
> It comes in Paris too
> As our lovers sing,
> In deserts has not much to do
> But comes; on tundras, from the ice
> Under the ground it works
> A ravelling lace of blooms. I am not nice
> In my desires so there but break some flowers in our parks.

When my friend came to Ayoda the Jews served notice and broke
From bondage; bombs rocked the carnival thrones; the kings, the hard
czars
Were split and emptied; the people like brains foamed through the
crack;
Truth rolled down cities in a tank, guns battering homes and stores
Of human hands to trash; I saw Farouk in his barque
Hide under the rails, and generals beat their drums and march
Through Egypt, Syria, sweet France, Washington, with sound trucks
and the works
Gladdened to plant new planets and give the old a lurch.

A fulcrum moves the world
I heard: and if it cry
As metals that we weld
Cry, fish and flesh must cry
Melting within us, burning to be still,
No matter. I have seen Troy
Town come up from fire whole
And Spring step there and die.

When my friend came to Ayoda he rode once more in Troy,
In Jerusalem battled, surrounded and back to back
Near his Maccabee brothers, at Charlemagne's side to try
A holy empire he strove; no mold in history broke
But he was there to break it. I say he lives now
In Troy and Jerusalem as here; the trees flower again
At his sole touch; Spring is not crumbled, not scattered, though
It flourish in gusts, in flurries of passion, and weary soon.

Though it weary soon
Friend, I have seen it come
In tumbling cities, seen it gone.
Friend, is it the same,
Concurring street and garden, waste
And Paradise, or only a repeat
Performance? Friend, is Eden lost
And come once more, or what we always greet?

When my friend came to Ayoda he brought in Plato's year
When all false forms were blown out; only their truth came
In Troy as here, and that relentless Republic tore
All loyalties but love alone. This is their doom
Who know that absolutes are true. What truth the myths bear
Is here and now. I shall love always, though I burn
For love's truth; though I burn my love for truth, I fear
No loss of loving; the wind cannot blow out his return.

Friend, is a constant thing
True always or again?
Sure, on the tundra Spring
Resumes his willing reign;
But love once burnt, who can remodel her;
Or once reborn in the millennium
Does she concur with absence or recur
In time: is she the same?

When my friend came to Ayoda love galloped a lilting reign;
Kings foundered as their lands, as gardens to the plough
Furrow and turn, as the earth gallops and rolls, as the nebulae spin
New worlds from gas to charity, as the suns and bent winds sow
Planets and seeds. Appearances melted, were sucked through valves,
Left truth lying undented, softer than force could hurt,
Unmoved, thinner than mass could pull; men made themselves
As fires, as Spring comes always to the gentle heart.

> Oh Rama my beloved
> As love comes always, long
> Delayed and never dead;
> As I burn now for Spring
> And grudge no mortal fire so it heat
> Old ground to break with fruit;
> I shall not trouble if love be the same
> So love but come.

SIR THOMAS MALEORE, KNIGHT

Better for this: who stand
(not as we) at the end
of a line, and yet believe
the others live,

Keep bright their meaning: pride
as no other pride heard
in a word: though silence be hard,
say not the loth word—

The loth word: call it loth,
word whose one force is faith:
What but a list of rules
tempered our schools,

But a game of scholars' wits
tilting with alternates,
balanced the world to come
on an axiom:

Granted: let this be true
that a word can make us true
or (call it loth) in a fall
unmake us all:

We are such things as words
are made on: the scholars' creeds
will fire our steel from faith
though the word be loth—

Better for this: who wrote
that a word could make us right,
that a dream could be our pride
and a game our creed.

OVER THE BOARD

the sun's under cover, working to rise
the opening: elements, swell of yeast, smell of bread
world without end in ferment, gambit, brew
you my love who analyze

agon all night bent over the board, what new line found
unseen till now, what ten-move trap, what mate?
move slowly: you shall see all
variations lose, all sacrifice unsound

(give all you have) when the sun bursts hot from the ovens shall rise
combinations: particles, the seeking blind, the eating dead
(and follow me) ten moves deep, pawned for you,
the white squares weak, centers torn, the radiant bellies bloat,
                                  split, under the eyes

the navel gaping hunger an unfilled mouth.
grandmaster of atomies: answer a rook, a queen, gamble, give all—
from rank phalanx and file the night
riders in scorn of order and breaking their leadlined squares will
                                                                    bound.

you my love who analyze
(agon   worldwrack   kingsfall)
the ones who cannot see two moves ahead
shall be their bread.

POSITIONAL

the game is made
of tension, white set
against black, my mind
against the clock. I move
by the book. each move I make
must own both name and sign
and change the line
of force for me
or for my enemy.

      but I dream
      while the clock holds my time
      in escrow, of a game
      that I could win
      in one sharp break.
              unforeseen.

            give all: the gallant throw
            their lives away, and still
            lose nothing; beggars sing
            and my book lists

                    the ways to lose a piece
                                save a world.
                    I hear the pieces cry
                    "abandon, sacrifice
                    destroy
                                this time for time
                    to come,
                                we are not all."

but how the lines insist
"we are your force
use, use, observe the rules,
avoid all loss,
reserve, conserve, invest
maneuver, twist.
let nothing go,
take no risk.
the strongest blow
strikes last
        move too soon and you lose
all.   for the beggar cries
'give' still
        though the sacrifice
were more than worlds of line
and balanced force contain
        or book define
and though you lose
        the rules remain."

                    i cannot reconcile
                    the heart's pull
                                and the mind's
                    sane bind.

for Max

TALE TO SLEEP ON

Let that evil lady
the Witch of Hindustan
Come out of the cave she shared
a deviltry ago
with the Wild Man
of Borneo.
Let her tell him, if she dare,
how the years have found
a touch to file
his ragged teeth to sand
a caress to bend
the roughest animal face
into a mask of civilized
and mannered grace.
He, if he heed this story,
may tell her with a smile
how day can add to day
a smoothness not foreseen
in any recipe
she used when with a bone
she stirred the devils up

distilled and poured and sipped
and ground to dust the cup.
Sinking on her knee
in ritual dignity
let her not lament
this timely fall, but bow
and shyly offer
him a draught not brewed
for any graceless quaffer:
the gift to see
how I who once in plain
enchantment marveled at
her polished, pointed claw
his toothy, animal grin,
exulting that
such monsters could be dreamed,
now in my waking am
those Powers I did enact:
the evil Dame, the Wild
Man of Borneo
joined bone to bone and vein
to vein in their embrace
in me, and ripe to ride
this galloping bloodtide
of daemons, freed from the tame
enjoyment of a child.

RHYME FOR THE CHILD AS A WET DOG

The hands that eased my mother's labor drew
Me out of a sure thing,
Cut the dream through, knotted it, then threw me
Onto a day of straw.

And the days I run yapping and hungry, ears
Flapping under the sky
That gives no orders, are happy;
The nights are one long

Run on a lawn where the rabbits' ears and the birds'
Beaks spring up like grass;
And in no hole, under no tree, chained up in no yard, around no
                                           daybreak
Corner lurks the big black

Half-wolf to worry my heels with bite of his night-
Call, or howl out how
Tonight I'll hold down the big job, take the long run on command,
                                        tomorrow let fall
The rabbits' ears, the birds' beaks /
                        on call.

A DENIAL

You say the white
Light   broken is not white
Any more, that if it pass
Through glass
It splits apart.
Then is the black
Night   broken, no
More night
Or no more black?
No
If a star break
The night, it is to show
The night more black
Around it. If my lips break
Silence, the silence will come back
More thick
With more to crack

Than sound can.
If my touch break
crystals of ice
Needling into your skin
When I have done
You won't know
Where I am.

for Jimmy

MATERIALS

now, if your lips had been made of ice they might tell
in melting, what our love is and yet lie:
ice melts and is still water; deserts run dry
but cannot syphon the tears out of the well;
the snail in his shell rots to water / his shell
remains; love is a form that cannot die;
though your soul drain away your jelly eye
will leave me a skullhouse charnel sentinel.
the form of love will keep you / when rains
muddle your lips the form of love will give
in ice and in chiseled silence one love-cry
fierce as the deathshead sun bursts our eyes / drains
the living jelly out so shape may live
/ frozen, melting, empty, quick to lie.

turn over and lie still: each way you turn
tells me how fixed our center is: we turn
like wheels, like worlds, like rope in one fast turn
about that mast whose firm stance cannot turn
but holds love past force of life, tide to turn.

or say: our love will tear as flesh must turn
with too long keeping; it is the wrestler's turn
Time tricks us with to throw us turn and turn
about, turn coat, tail, collar—oh no turn
of mind or wit will keep you fast when turn
you must. lie still: we're snails and we must turn
houses out of our flesh; music and turn
about one constant note heard past its turn
in the mind's silence where all notes return.

how long our note is held yet not to stay
my mind from keeping time; our first note, begun,
will fall out of thought before the last is done
/ the small change i count is all my pay.
how i lose promise in performance, say
word after word / let the words outrun
my running brain; no counterpoint or pun
is so rich in strength to last in this relay.
i stay, and it's moments, moments i can make
love that is music hold time till we sleep.
out of our neck and neck quick heat of skin
on skin, note on note, word on word, yes, take
what goods you can, love; you'll have nothing to keep,
more than a moment to keep measure in.

Time has known more of me than you have known.
measure of my lips to yours, our hearts' exchange,
what our loves keep / what they rearrange,
what our bodies write / into us inmost the bone:
cell, marrow, sloughed off, regrown: this you know, call your own.
Time / measures not the passion but the change.
you count my depth of love, Time takes my range

for record, and that book is a coffer of stone.
this page is yours / sure as i made it for you,
no other, for this instant heartbeat / i give
you instant, instance, yet make no instant live.
though i shout love aloud, you hear, it's no more true.
love's measure in me lives, the words alone
unblurred by their motion, my breath / caught in stone.

before you build me a house let all clocks warn
you in your clicking instant what you do:
you have cut no wood / worms cannot wind through,
found no shell but water winks in it; houses of horn
our music swells in will empty, our reeds lie torn
to echo silence. were it our guts we new-
tuned over our coffins, they'd shake themselves untrue
each note less keen, at the last, pitch flat outworn.
no music sounds but for the silence sings
around it: call us boxes, we live filled
with emptiness for quavers to be trilled
in, and that shaking outburst breaks our strings.
my body is all your house, though it won't last
one rest around your death, the long note past.

number the frequencies of joy, how one
shock added has made a higher note of it,
how brasses have set new tones, dead wood has set
round us boxes our living airs may overrun,
how the rub of your bow on my rosin is respun
now (stroke hair on hair) in music, our breath is knit
with no-breath, our plucked nerves know / to transmit
harmonics, the fabric surfaced, struck, laced with the sun.
count out aloud the measures, name the scales

play us: death and your body give them voice.
we are in what stays when all music is destroyed,
in the web, in the dress, in the shiver of space as it fails,
in the shake of stretched cords in our emptiness, that choice,
the hollow hunger mouthing our hearts, the void.

if this quaint instrument with which you toy
to trill your pleasure might be more than box
you might be more than cord, more than word: shocks
of air displacing air that airs employ
to sound out silence. if my song destroy
song, note by note, word after word sense mocks
itself, keys sprout discordant from their locks,
Rome has no room in it we can enjoy.
that powerful rhyme how much plays false, sounds forced
since tongues first waggled Rome and room apart?
of Chaucer's racketing innocence, believe
what lost, you, since our ear, his tongue, divorced?
does this word box hold keep translate my heart
promised: thou shalt have queynte enough by eve?

materials will melt, that sweet machine
corrode wherein i ticked out words for you.
love will change color, time at work turn hue
itself to a memory, the half, the mean
response to truth; all music will come clean
of melody, all measure tap untrue.
this (i tell you) worst of all work our mouths can do:
words, by their changing, change what love must mean.
this language which alone holds what i feel
for you when our love is altered will not keep.
the sound will sift, it will change taste as our tongues trip,

shed shape as our bodies molder, rust away from its steel
precision; though we made love out of words alone,
asleep, lip on lip melts, mumbles the life from the bone.

when our music has found new soundingboards, when our shade
and color turn, when our tones, sung in some new shell,
reach new pitches, when change in our alloy changes the bell
we were (as it must), let your fingers search the dust made
poets, musicians / those lost motes that played
pun, counterpoint, invention, villanelle.
recharge the force of their atoms, tell them to tell
what song tongues sing in us when words are in earth laid.
shall i not be remembered, love; shall i
not be remembered? love, think that when we're dust
and English changed, men of science will come to find charts
in these lines, plot relationship, figure the turning lie
of your shape against mine, the thrust, friction, current of lust
love's structure in us when tension has left the parts.

learn of me magic for you may not find
another who has science to move you so.
Time when i touch you will tick out fast or slow
desire ripple in you as your rivers wind.
space will not hold you, your heart not be confined
in any cage of rib or will but go
unrhythmed, as motes in the sun, atoms (quicksand) go
devouring power to loose, power to bind.
you shall taste how the currents flow in you
unchanged from lead to gold, chained by that spell
mass shouted when sun, when moon, sudden / crashed to a standstill,
love, death, on the instant, fixed, melting, the seas let through
an army, that thunder of blood in us might tell
how the red tides closed in to make their kill.

TWO

LA NATURE MORTE DE SAMUEL BECKETT

1   Beckett to Seated Figure

The red hair
That extrudes itself from the tumescent nipple
Of the seated figure in the picture
Is not less unimportant
Than the seated figure in the picture
Whose expression, as has been noted,
Is one of strain.
If I strain, costive
In the equilibrium of all that I deny,
To express these figures
Of dead men straining at a chord, a hair, a stool, a frame
Of what moves before them, to hold it still
Until
They can see what it is
That moves, and if it is
What lives, am I
Less than they?

2   Seated Figure to Beckett

Blooming, thanks, and you
Brooding, thanks, and you
Brooding too?
I expected better of you
Who knew
Before you moved the first piece
Out of safety, into passion
That the only sound move
Is a stasis.
Let them count with you
In that pillory of dust which is their station
Where only the eyes legitimately may move
The infinite variations of position
For the seated figure in the picture
Who no matter how you place him will still look
Into himself and unpleasing to them.
For the seated figure in the picture
Asks no more of you
Than that he be permitted to continue
To strain at a chord, a hair, a stool, a frame
A fugue of the variations
Which can be made out of the soul's death
And the will's unending motion
Till his bowels burst.
The figure asks no more of you
Than the crowd ask, who pause
Before making their move
To stare at the seated figure in the picture,

To laugh, sneer, retch, yawn, to proclaim their thanks
That you stick to still life and don't try to do portraits
Of people they might know.

3   Beckett to Seated Figure

I am not concerned with description
So much as with placement.
The standing figures outside
The picture, who stare with such persistent loathing
At the seated figure in
The picture, do not see
The frame or me
But none the less they see
What I must show, and they
Find that they must pay
Exactly what I ask
For the privilege of being shown.
And the figure in its infinite variations
Shuffling its stone soul from pocket to pocket
In the delusion of death
Is still
Life.

CAME THE TERRIBLE DARK LORDS

of everything movable in their cars
the steam drills shouting
through the skin
into the dark steam drill places
of everything
            in their cars

built up from scratch
it was not what you thought it was

CONSTRUCTION

what you think now you will think then
what you think then you will have thought
a hundred years from then in your carriage
with your horse and your fine rig
your striped pig the prize
granted articulacy

come to me
when the sun is not alone
in pain and the sky
but everyone
                let
me force my silence on you shout
into your tongueroots my black bit
nothing blot
world between the teeth
                        tell how dreamed
my mindmen as i did
of minds gone dry lips
paid out all words sucked from them split
scratch any surface you'll find this

BREAK

hung out to shrivel the order
of words a matter of drill
                        the king who rent
my sackcloth membrane with his lament
riding his chariot backwords the sage
hardened in marble halls

                        this
is your Invoice
please keep it clean

LAST NIGHT WHEN YOU WEREN'T
HERE

at the door   the visitor
who comes when the blood is away who was not you, scratched
his clawed hand shaking
gold hair of the chandelier
down. there was no place   (beautiful
there was no time   the golden
         orator the singer / no
right rhyme. i tried
to tell you but i couldn't
who stood at the door who wouldn't
come in who wouldn't let
me out   there was no way

it happened that i spoke to you
when the blood was away and what
i said was what you knew   the rhythm
of words in me
who wouldn't come into me who wouldn't come out of me
went out of me
was what went out, was what was left

(beautiful the golden
singer the oriole hair
bird shaking, the bird of seasons

was what would not be changed
when we were dead

(the bird
of absences, the visitor

across the space in my blood

THE NOISE

outside the window
wasn't a noise, it was so constant, went on,
wasn't outside the window just because
it was a noise outside, was that so much
it was my mind hummed to you, it was
what i had to say, it was the wheels
inside the wheels in me.

say i am all that to you then, Columbus:
Avenue to a world they all pour through
to reach it, this poem
you must run through / while
it runs through you
to hear it.

i should have liked
to say to you one thing that no one else

had said, to do for you one thing
that only i could do, to be here

                              in you

and have you say
true

NO PLACE I'VE BEEN

has been like this
everywhere that i am / i can see as far
as the crystal palace where
garbage can lid moons clang out
the dead man's jangle

            it was not
            like this when that lust
            at the heart of all lust banged out of me
            in a clatter of things used
            bric-a-brac
                        filigree
            elegant wasteful coquetry

let's / boast
of what we can't keep
it can all be tossed away
and not change what we are

THREE-MAN BLUES

new york woman
with my safety glass
with my broadbeamed head-
lights i talk of death
my chrometrimmed tail-
finned belly purred
the loins turned over
wherever i ran
this coffeebreak year
i felt the black man
with a big meat cleaver
my old coat
what i want isn't much
turned inside out
but there's a big bag
that i won't touch

and where i was
Patrice came too
with a beadstring grin

and a thick fun fur
overstated
bedraggled and soiled
and a sunburst pin
and the dreams came too
immoderate
when he was dead
many and many
the nights were oily
i came with him
all greasy and smelly
safe underground
in the lion's belly

the vulture's mouth
my jackal bed
where i took cover
and wild and woolly
Malcolm came after me
with a big red fez
torn open and had
again and again
give it more juice
get out fast
don't want to make noise
for those bad men

don't want to see
where i run to
banana hairy
jungle unruly
and god damn rough

from his coffeebean cover
Che spurts up
every neighbor will hear
this woolly pelt
yell fear
have pity on me
don't let me handle
don't break me down
this brown gold black-
belt war / fare
this dirty gorilla
face hair

the big black birds
tumble my bed
how many more
that i don't love
before next year
will i cry for
purr over

and where i am
i must lie down
with Che

DEATH BY VIOLENCE

with string beards, fur in disarray
let them speak for themselves, build up,
the hairy heroes of history,
the attraction. if we sat down
together, the tape
spinning, the scourges of God,
to talk, would they say: glamor
i had a ball: no
consumer

                        there wasn't much
can afford to be without
no mess no grease
this   *and what there was*
in ivy-curtained hall, in jungle wall
                was minimal
look up, tell me

                it makes your hair lie flat
if we could live long
this way

THE SACRIFICE

1

a savage in me shakes
somewhere back of the heart
on a stick a mess of charred
skins bones rattles and hopes
that because of the blood spoken
in Memphis, the word we need,
love, will shout, loud
and hardy as any weed. say
that red drink creates the cup
to contain it, that bribe makes
the good will hold true. say
that i in my ordained pride
will build from him, drink him up

                                       or all

the old rituals lie.

2

but myself / to tell it out, how count how, with what words
make for you, out of the bedrock, that city
spring? easier and more grateful, from the bug bit me
last night construct the whole race of insects, from the furred
bush your hand brushed then make up a mind. hard
to sell to you what i've not seen but just felt hit me
again, not even a blueprint, a pattern: the chance that we let be
in us what, when say it, how loud we know, can't be heard.
not from him, buried with never so good a word, will,
prayer, heart's choice, can any good break. plough him
down deep, forget him, plant no more there, but furrow me
over as last night or then with every tear, all will
to make me yield all up. it is at home
in all places, in all men, or not at all, that city of man will come,
bloody, as it has been, and leaping up, not to be told no, in you, in me.

"I hate black people." —Miranda, 5 years old, on a bus

POEM FOR MY TWO DAUGHTERS

well ok study / the art at your mirror, how
to get out of yourselves, go tune
round banjo hands to the key of it, jump up today
with a wiggle in Warsaw Miranda and sullen shine
your hips up to Prague late afternoon and on
through the Tonkin sunset baby you're a big girl now

           love five
years into us / let the moon snap
black garters. my girls go down tonight
                (faces old for the cut of your bones, don't fit
                                      right
cold of a city sickness: some bastard banged shut
Alison your small obstinacies
                (foot pats / the floor, won't move till
                there's nobody tells it to, then swoops way
                high in my lastyear stiletto-heeled laugh
                    some damn
fool / burnt / out
your hands on my armstrings

(silver away quick, won't let
no dance music play with you till you're dead
                                        sure
it won't lump big-bellied in Biafra

            yes, polished, all set to shoot
the sun right back at you, look, here she stands, smiles
Miranda, with your sly, coaxing lips next door
west 93rd street the last stoop down
                (makes mean
mouths
                and it's at herself / shouts
white girl get out
with your wise mouth

SCIENCE

it's dead, you said, love
a learned response, a cry

is no more
of strings to play

cry for a word?
more human than grief
since the first word stood up
shed blood
for you to build on
at chopwork
no word's hand

the tears you let go
laugh at you
no word has burnt wood
bones that were laid down
no word has killed
in time's rough surgery
has been skilled

but for this, yes
some words took sick
why there lived words once
power to shout out
and any fool hear

if you like, cry
and may die
(you'd not believe it) had
till they made stars break
what they were good for

underground

or not what words were.

ALL MUD

the road
wheel ruts hip thick and the track
hard going. i was hard put
to carry all that
freight jigs promises jolts thrills
sun moon up down frost heaves
forever
                my head rolled
the weight   the touch
of your mind on me made
the wheels stick
                    came back
joints loose eyes unhitched
from the pole turning
through me   you
who forget the new day
        it won't be so much
        as a pinprick
before dawn
think of me think of me
who junked one morning

FOR DYLAN THOMAS

look, your nerve-ends are stroked off
for the encounter
your voice sloughed
with the golden hunter
when you slip under
the roots of trees, go through
the force behind the weather
under the roots of eyes

as your blood in these words crawls
blind through narrows of rhetoric as
                    orator don't be fooled
your voice strokes now
the voice that's in the feather
(through nothing, that thundered
nothing)

          the windy magic in the grave
the death that's in the flutter
of the bowels:
not theirs but yours

THIS POEM MAY NOT BE JUST WHAT
YOU WROTE TO SANTA FOR, BUT

look, no ornaments. did you ever see
such a plain cold bareboned creature to be your thing
for a minute or how long? when you got up this morning
you were, i'll swear it, on edge, impatient to see
what the day would unwrap for you. / this time, see
sweetheart, no new image, no odd symbol, no turning
away from the one thing given. / anything
i give you, if you don't like it, get rid of me;
if you don't get it, you don't get me. and then,
if you get it, you still don't get me. i'm not here
where you think i am. i'll swear you think i'm in
the words i say, but i'm in them and all here
only the way thunder is in a drum:
you've got to strike it to make that surface boom.

SORRY, SWEETHEART,

                                      here's
another, a jumping, a clumsy,
big / bouncing / loud
all over you just like somebody
else's eager dog,
rough / red / tongue
out and the thick turned-down-
at-the-corners lips / letting a gusher
spatter your jacket, poem.
                      you've struck it today
out here in the hallway, don't have to come in, you wanted
something, had in mind someone
then, when you married me, graceful
fine haunches, could give tongue gently,
exact
                          (no turmoil, lost slippers, bones out in the
                                      garden
                    bigmouth loudmouth blabbermouth yammerer

could make comfort lie down
with you and not get riled

           (but this, too, hates to hurt, tries too hard to
                                   please,

        paws, full of mud,
        up on you, it will come
        when it wants, won't do as you choose

MUSICK FOR A REEL OR
A ROUND DANCE

my nails were tapping yesterday
against the wall, and i thought of you,
all by themselves, as i used to do,
as it used to be, without meaning to.

we had forms that worked for this kind of thing
once: each flesh had its roundelay;
to refrain, we knew, was as good as to say
again what the time in us had to say
and the jiggle of death in us made us sing
    it will come again, it will come to stay
what the shake of our bodies threw away
      and we moved and kept still without meaning to.

MY MIND SHOPS FOR DESIRE

After thirteen years the novelty wears off.
My eyes measure you and I feel no curious
Itch to uncover what shall be with us
When tongue cut to tongue and loin to loin we rough
New patterns for old pleasures out. That stuff
Well-sewn, your skin, grows to me without fuss
Or ruffle and simple and easy as what in us
Moves without special hurry. It is enough
That wearing you like a dress I wear out time.
Surely (as sometimes I half-see, in haste, one, light's
Trick on him, glamor of stance, makes parade, turns
That shift my mirror my mind to hold up dreams:
Fresh fashion and hurry) I lust for lust when right
Fit, sureness, fast reflex, you, habit of love, lie on me and make me
                                                            yours.

DANCE POEMS

1

when you go dear
take your arm around
with you.
you'll have to go back
if you forget.
you'll have to come down
to where he is.
the man says so.
don't worry about his head
just go.

2

the joining of hands: the bodies
slide under the hands
the girl up, the man down
the man up, the girl down
and when they find a way

to be there
one moves, one is still.

3

under the gothic arms' arch
it's easy to make anything
into the nave of the high legs
move   /   stippled
lit in the rising steeple
of feet
        if you don't move
as it's easy to move, don't bend
as it won't strain
to bend, don't lean
so soon: tell me what falls
if you lean, if you get the hands joined
before the end seems set
to begin

note: part 1 is an assemblage of the ballet master's instructions to his dancers.

AT AVIGNON

As that way it happens, the gentlemen on the stone
Bridge over the river bow, and the ladies bow,
Each knowing the moves; as this way, sweetheart, and now
You take me the same old country, the old road
Through the same furred thicket, that travels the same known
Journey, to take our positions, pose, bow
To the artist who set it all up: oh / now
Let him take our likeness, for long it will not hold.
Here on the bridge that dancing leads nowhere
(Turns to no more than an old song) take my hand;
Tell me how knowing the music hums we're here
Where we've been before will fire you as you stand
To turn me and shake with me, break with me out of it, where
The stiff dancers go when they break their cold round.

THREE

JUST

yesterday, sitting
with you, eating
grapefruit, a word i'd stuck
too hard or at the wrong angle squirted
tart into my eye.

talk of love, always, yes, like that,
your bristles up, the hairs on your neck
stiff, sharp as your voice, what is it
makes you take love so hard?

TWO CATS ON A WALL IN FLOODTIME, HONEY, AND

nothing to talk about but myself and no
self to talk about to you: lay a finger
on anything looks like mine it won't be there
put anything into me it will slip right through
love, take anything out of me, it was you
planted it, made it stick / some / other
time when we both knew what I was for
made me be what i had to be for you.

come with me, this is the same old alley-cat
scramble we went at spitting yesterday
what love you use to hold me, i am wet
quick for you, inside my skin turn, slither away
make floods rise to you and laugh when they run out
when all that heat you throw into me / won't stay.

THE PACT: THREE SONGS

1

i came here
to drink with you
because you asked me to
but let me warn you now
i don't trust you
i think you're going to drink me
i think you mean
to suck my mind out then
crush me, drop my shell
in a bag with things to be
burnt. i guess
you want to use me
to keep yourself warm
i came here to use you
meaning no harm.

2

let me give you all
my uglies on one plate
when you flick the light on
    well, where i come from
i hang out black
cloths on all
the squares that let light out
    there were no
    such things as feathers, moon
when you bring seed
for me / *no wings no sky*
i want to be free
when you make
yourself at home here / *no*
    such thing as home
    where i went to
i say why did you come / *where*
    there was nothing planted
    firmly i could see
when you talk love
my toes curl tight
around my hate / you ask me for
    no roots to hold, no tree
    to stand on, make me sing
something beautiful
    the changes in a thick pool
    coming out of me
to keep i tell you
please just let me sleep

3

cat's-eye stone
brown and gold
the wolfman gave to me
here the colors curl mixed
like all good things in me
full moon blanches nose and cheek
leaves my eyeholes dark
my hands
whistle over you
each place they touch
goes black

cat's eye man
behind closed doors
my room smells warm
when you lie
across my belly, try
to make my back forget
how all along
the cold sheet rubs
that marries me
to earth

MOUTH LIKE A CACTUS (a folktale, how charming)

all greeny and spiny
there once was a lady prickly with promise
tongue of tabasco she tickled you
into the sauce of grace
and on the red premise of time for all killings cooked up reasons
eager as onions to sting you from rest
will of hot curry, the pungent desire to see no comfort, lust of
                                                  mixed pickles
her thighs could open wider than hundreds of settlement cookbooks
                                                     laid end to end
snap shut like a mind

now easy as loving and lazy as ever
no season so gentle with gelatine breasts
but puffed in her omelettes of death
and in applepie order she rose / graceful with garlic to whip up
                                                     quick
menus of murder all spicy and juicy to make you go down just right
when no one was looking sliced out counters

of thought to shout
> *you roach*
> *oh what shall i do in the blandness of summer*
> *where you lie steaming to gobble me up*

and laid / tables past hope
> with *where shall i tarry with what salt sprinkle*
> *what brainbrine keep you tonight*

from the aspic jungle where lazy
as lonely is, easy as losing one day
one musical bubble she uttered before
closed over her oceans of jello and deep
in your bowels she was heard no more

". . . Never had I more
Excited, passionate, fantastical
Imagination . . ."

　　　　　—*Yeats*

　　　　　　　　　　for my grandmother

WHAT WOULD YOU SAY, THOUGH

if that fantastical
imagination had died before the man:
if all that rage and all that pride
were rags a squawling child wore out:
put on the mind as dress, take off
reason, hang it there on the hook

　　　　　　　　　　go back

to what you were before
the mind was buttoned on;

　　　　　　　　if

that old lady made knots for hours together
to tie up a doll would be herself, and pulled
out all the knots again, made a new self,
the old self, a squealing crying wanting
pity of self for itself?

　　　　　　　to make it
that way were easier than bring back
life and all those days to get
through mumbling /

　　　　　　　　what she forgot

ARRANGEMENT FOR VOICES

One: Duet

the girl who is in her twelfth year
will play the most difficult . . . the boy
who is not yet seven will

                   in Saltzburg

                   work was a burden. I could hardly
perform on clavichord or harpsichord; he will also play
a concerto for viola, will
accompany symphonies   when I play

                the audience are all tables
                and chairs
                the keyboard
covered with cloth, as easily
as if he could see the keys

                  the voice of nature
                speaks loud in me louder
                than in many a strong lout
                the boy
will instantly name all notes played
at a distance singly or in chords on clavier

or any instrument—bell glass or clock. he
will improvise as long as desired
in any key   I cannot
                    live / as young men do these days

                    Two: Fugue

I still owe eight
ducats, am not
able to pay you, but
my trust in you is so boundless that
I dare ask you to help me out
with a hundred

                              you desire
                    an opera from me. If you intend
                    to stage it at Prague, I cannot
till next week. Great
God I wouldn't wish my worst
enemy covered with cloth
as easily

                              my operas
                    inseparable from the company
                    for which I wrote
my wife my children, all depends
on whether you will lend me
another five hundred   never
                    produce their calculated effect
                    for God's sake
forgive   it would be another
                    matter to write a new opera for your
                                        theater. Even then

        I am obliged to
resort to money-lenders excretory

pylitis pyonephritis spread the news
I'm willing
     to give lessons

                  Three: Requiem

accompany symphonies at a distance
in chords covered with cloth and latent
focal lesions the kidneys
inescapably   risk
              to put myself
              in competition with the great
              Mozart. If i could
              fill every lover of music
              with feelings as deep, comprehension as clear
              as my own in hearing
        the boy
on any instrument—bell glass or clock
                    Prague
              must keep this treasure
as long as desired
in any key   but not without fit
              reward. The want of this
eventual   total
nephritic insufficiency. I am
wretched couldn't sleep last
night. Can you not
help me? The smallest sum
tables and chairs and the queen
of the night on bell glass clock
trills cut-up noodles   as clear
              as my own, covered with cloth

                    inseparable from every lover
                    of music
                            my   hour
on   bell   glass   clock   in
any   key   strikes
before I can prove my talent / I am writing
at a distance
                this requiem
                        for myself
and see the keys, can state
the counter-theme   all
notes played in me / life
was beautiful

  note: this poem is made of excerpts from journals, letters, etc. Most
of the mediation has been in the arrangement. The second voice in parts
two and three is Haydn's.

ALICE TO WILLIAM JAMES FROM KENSINGTON

– – – – – – – – –
the leaves peel off
                    dead skin
                              flakes
                                     down
                                           snow
dear brother you overdo
in my commonplace the tragic
it will not stick
this year there will be no
white cover   don't think of me
                           as a creature who might have been
                           something else
no thick
      /
        blanket
of what i was laid down

the progress as simple now
in my body as any fact
of nature
          each
                    step
what i wanted.

————————————————————

this year
if you had walked round my death
not up to it
               my leaves
                         would have missed you
my skin cover

                              i'm working as hard as i can
                              to get dead as soon as i can
                              but what to die of
                                              or how
                              we're
                                   to live
                                          through
the first night i don't know
applause sprouts from each window, my
brain
     flakes
          home

——————————————

                              if i die in my sleep, not
                              to be one of the audience will
                              kill me.

since
i've been here i've wanted some real
disease to pick off, some real
self to die of. you
haven't been
            can't know
                the relief

                        dry, leaf after
                                leaf in
me, as i crisp
into the deep city
hum of sustained concrete
symptoms at last laid down   in my body
                fall
to hold me   simple now
— — — — — — — — — — — — — — — — —
                        my best peels off, the grand
                        mortuary moment so near
                        to put me to sleep will bore
                        the audience.
he'll come
once this week
                measure
/ how deep my cover
then we'll all / die

                    a natural death, thick

104

           as simple as any fact

           my substance,
                       can't

           of nature

           in my body

           be dug out

———————————————

note: much of this poem is made of excerpts from the letters of Alice James to her brother. I have changed some words and invented others for her, but most of my mediation has been to provide an arrangement, a frame, and the statement that this is a poem.

THING IS

we add it on, we add on skin
to the cold bones / call them
beautiful   hair, nails onto the bare
animal   that's what makes it
viable   /   paste
nostrils over the nose hole, say it can
breathe in, breathe out, say it was made
to do that.
              under the feet
a floor, go on, over the hair
no   more   bare
sky, inside the zero house
the mouth, not cold now, heat, a clod
of air swarming / loud we bang
it on, rap out
the word the name the man
                        sense
      (howl   /   all   /   around
        the idiot central sound /
hammer

HOLY SONNET

Not the defense, not the characters of love, not the affair
Not the whole floating opera, the golden notebook, new directions
                                                    seventeen
Marble, the gilded monuments, the magic christian, who over me
                                                    gravely stare
Leer, pirouette, cavort (these damn books dare put me down)
Pinnacled dim in the intense evergreen
(See how the distances shake me, the sixties will none of me) watt
                                                    then will cure
My affliction, bring me salvation? Invisible man pray for me here
On the shelf of the shadow of death under the celebrant palms of
                                                    literate sin.
Look at me, I am dying of terminal
Conjunctivitis, the itch for connections, too much rouge in the eye
Listen, varicose ears, hardening of the brain howl in me, sunflowers
                                                    suture me, here in me al-
Ways won't let me pray
Grant me, forebears and confrères, no gas in the heart
May it befall me, even as your saints, to achieve the spontaneous
                                                    remission of all my warts.

FOUR

LAMENT

when we were
easy to love we lay under millions
of dollars and played with them and let them
cherish us. they liked to
live with us. we made them
at home. now we hear them
whimpering all day
behind the curtains and in dark
corners. we've become
translated, a far land
no millions like to travel
or old or used.
serious /
          they've forgotten how
to smile at us
talk of fidelity. money
only plays with shiny
new people

MEETING

he says a poem is
he says a poem is
a poem this is not
a poem he is not
a poem in any sense

he says (holy jumping sacred
purple cows) the passion
for exclusion rides him
again, makes him dance, sing
a poem, a monkey through my
hair / jabbering

ok poet man
make it how you can
i won't let you in
if you won't let me in

THE HANDSOME MAN

doctor oh doctor pick me up
/ my handsome man
take me away in that little black box
doctor oh doctor oh word doctor
thought doctor / book doctor
world reader with choosy eyes
doctor lock me up
in your worm-free well-wrought holding box
the way i used to be
measure my loins to see they fit
measure my skull, measure it
classify the slant of my voice
the tone of my eyes and where they fit

doctor oh doctor be very sure
what it is you've got
word plumber / soul scanner
oh / star / reader
try to be sure as sure
that what you've caught can never get out

with its heart in its plumeting paths of hands
its rocketing hands, its trail of fire
lolloping hands to run amok
and gobble you up, gobble you up
/ my handsome man

MURALS BY MAGRITTE

In the casino at Knokke-le-Zoute

the green on four sides
will eat the house
and be a man. the house
gets into the tree. the frigate sails
through the chandelier
and through the chandelier

out of the fish-lady
to the man with doves in his rib-cage.
the tower the pen and the horn
and the girl with the doves
turn into a worm later on
turn into a worm later on

that is a tower that is
a horn the green on four
sides eats the house and
the feathers fall from the dove
and the feathers fall
from the dove

FOR CAROLYN

     she
has said what the heart thinks
and she is in difficulties
she has sung what the mind grasps at
well, she must be discarded
she has danced that jiggle the blood holds
forget it, baby, she's not for you
she's howling here what the man knows
yeah, her ass is gonna come off right now

she has given what the grave takes
and she is not in difficulties

A READING GLASS

i still hold it against you
even though i've already told you
this, and we thought we'd canceled it, that in
the Memling Museum in Brugge, when i looked at
Christ's face through a reading glass you seemed to sneer
at such a concern for mere technique. that night,
drinking beer, you and i and our friend, he said what
to you was fact clearly stated, to me wit:
    Memling spent all that care
    to paint what was not there.

in this, if you like, i'll grant you the argument, admit
i take the wit and not the thought, as if
the surface and texture mattered. but it wasn't
the brushstrokes or anything near technique
i paid attention then / close to worship / more
a fidelity to what he knew, the labor
not unlike what we do,
when he squinted in candlelight through a reading glass
that seemed to bend all he saw. he looked through that blur

the eye unaided will make of what's there, set
down each braided hair
on the Virgin's head, made
each jewel a mirror to throw the invisible
real world of his painting back at you, each tear
a mirror, each pearl of sweat on the Crucified Man's
forehead. he gave you
by straining his sight what's there for the eye to see
though the brain in its cold sufficiency
to imagined, diminished truth can't take it
without a reading glass and humility.

that was your world you walked past, held away from you
as if detail were a corruption, as if to tell me,
take it away, that braided
hair will spoil
my purity.

if i'm not fair to you, hurt you, anger you,
i hurt myself, but what else to do if not
set down all i saw, as he did,
the lines tangled, crossing,
recrossing, and clear, clear
through my reading
glass?

I IMAGINE YOU

galloping home at five
in triumph, the breadwinner:
what ho, honey, i've done it again, we can eat,
the children can go to college
tomorrow

    (actually
  i imagine you
  careworn, patient, politely
  answering their nervous
  questions with a frown
  while you think of me, and your absent
  mind puts them down)

tell me i should be
above such thoughts, tell me love should make me high,
tie wings on my arms, fluff up the feathers,
carefully, carefully push me off
the barn roof: i am of those
who won't fly.

for Robert Creeley

MAN

hesitant.

everything in him
has walked across his face
in hobnailed boots
the cleats
lips
       nostrils
              eye

              now
                     gone. the boots
walk into you. they leave him
emptied.

NARROWS

put in your oar, you'll stir
a muddy bottom here, but not
take away my
resistance; it's what i
have, i hold it tight,
i know how to use it

              uses
              of a man and a woman, the uses
              of us, one to the other,
              as if to pull the worth
              out of us.

streams change / often
from year to year we
have to relearn the water.

you come to me who
need something to do
with me   if i go
              with you, if i
              answer, give you back

          a shifting outline, mirror
          what you don't know you know

    if we
love or don't love here or
farther on, what in us
can be lost
       only
by forcing we lose who know
to move in our perfect, tentative
rhythm, no haste no sparing
of nerve / no
smoothness no untruth

i say, boiling around
you, wishing i could
make that for you   balanced, hovering, still
                                 at the heart of the eddy transfixed
                                 unmoved, unmoving, you
                                   mirror of me
                                      move
we're neither of us stripped
of resources.

       say then
i am the skin comes
off you, wrung out / hung
on the line and the line
                    here
shaking / what
you give me is that.

WORD FROM THE BADLANDS

1

it's a question of heat / what it brings
to be worth the price of parching. yes. i'm happy.
millennia i've delayed telling my story
the air wasn't right, the words
too short, the space between
breathing and dying too long, no one ready.
when the sun stammered a haze
over my dust-dogged ridges i tried to sweat out
my poverty of spirit:
why it was i could not
make a *King* to ride these plains.

                    look
down, delay
twice, pause three times
in a magic circle before
to test your powers with fuse   (*Masked Man*
at the ready you make   (*Bandito*
your entry. out of my lack   (*Friend*
i've ground out dust for you.

                    2

what's my loss
Kid in you i don't know but it's
gorgeous, it bares teeth six feet tall.
if i don't air out the temple where it lies
it smells bad
                multiplies

                    forgive me, i didn't know
there were any alive who could bear the news: *Sweetheart*
i'm happy, you're wise, we love, it isn't enough.
now that the birds
hoarse shouts of praise, a beginning, uncertain, have circled
earthquake and tumbled hills, fed on bones laid bare
by our explosion / needles in glass caves quivered to register
the force / of your devotion
the table dried up, the water fallen
                            into exhaustion
to stagnate, to clog, to blister the gills of blind fishes with passion
                        of our corruption

in their far wells, i can contemplate
erosion, excavate
my mythology of hate.

what i've let burn was what i never had
what you've dug up was what no one should
the wealth of life i've carried has turned
cumbersome and vile
asleep in my sandpit, humps
his armor rubbed, his mouth burst
with gases, nostrils stuffed
with dust

       great reptile

          my love

CANYON

so
we'll reckon it up here
i thought well of myself
when jellyfish learned their soft
grey parasols into my brain
i / thought / much
of the good-try claws clipped
ghost of opposed thumb
toolgrip   axehaft
in their snap / thought
more of the crude jaw
the blunt teeth held
promise in them of this
l o v e b i t e

        (here
          thought most of you, true
          climax of every age)

                                   i use
                          the moments when i cut strata up
                          throw nothing out, gloss all
                          as i read you /
                                        dents in the wall

ask me what questions i'll tell you what dies
at the edge where the shadow knows

        i'm in love fast
        with every loud joke
        hot jock / can
        before tonight rock
        with the stoned dead in bed
        in their set teeth, with what
        rotgut can make me shake
        the same dead beat
        from the cold meat spread
        in the tables of rock

SAINTS

hanging on every wall. how do you like your saints, worn
down with their long temptation in the desert
but human / how
will you take your desert, plain, mudflat, a sandy
waste, or must it crawl with mind-monsters / will you
take them as they come /

                    Lord,
how dost Thou desire Thy saints to walk
this earth /

                tired, ugly
                foolish, mouths half open,
                one white, thick strand
                of drool dropped from each corner, cheeks
                sagging, lips pulled down
                by an epileptic fit / eyes
                vacant with contemplation /

or

you may in your mystic way only prefer them
to favor in stiff, unenviable regalia.
bearing gravely on gaunt foreheads the gifts that came
uneasily out of their struggles, they stagger
across and across the gold canvasses, one cold
star on each ridged brow. from each loose hand
dangles knife, rake, fork or tongs,
the martyrdoms they craved,
tongues torn out, eyes torn out, breasts held up
wet, glistening on gold salvers, even the sandy
deserts gold, the lions of Saint Jerome
gold too, although sometimes his lions have human faces.

should i say how
that lavish splendor wears my eye down till
i can't see the glory
for the gold

                              a frameful of gold
                              a wallful of gold
                              a spaceful of gold
                              a roomful of jewels
                              a handful of pearls
                              a crownful of sweat
                              a faceful of drool
                              a mouthful of tears
                              a headful of thorns
                              a heartful of death
                              all / shining

thus. they lived and died to tell
you, traveler, what /
                    the tired saint next door
the one who drools and has fits: even
you, you can be martyred too, I did it.
look at Me, it's that easy;
                    the stiff, painted
doll with its tongue in a casket screams at you:
look at the long strain,
the effort, the frenzy,
and the reward a thing
you can't imagine
or want / left
up to you / your baby.

for Paul Blackburn

FOUND

                       said

to me
      here

                     "a bloody mess

(from the torn thighs
to the ground   "and all that
                     "Venus
                     "Adonis

(the knotted cord
packed into the bowels

                     "and the return

oh sunflower weary

                     "to earth

(the cord jerked
out the shit
and the guts
ride with it   "to earth
where it's at

132

                          what should i make
of it   this
was given
        to me
            to trust

    note: some of this poem is assembled from things Paul said in
Aspen, '67

FOR MY FRIEND WHO HATES ME

you with your handsome machete
i with my polished box
you with your stake and mallet
i with my polished box
you with your incorruptible / fire
you with your tin ear
i with my polished box

i with my hungry moon
you with your full bullet
i with my hairy hands
you with your full bullet
i with my monster's / refusal to be real
i with my animal smell
you with your full bullet

you with your certain chisel
i with my closed rock
you with your winch and tackle
i with my closed rock

you with your lack of balance
you with your sight of glory
i with my closed rock

i praise God for you as for all
loved killers who go selfless and mad
dear as they must steadied by no
doubt that what they break must
break, what they lose must be
lost

    i with my polished
voice, i with my rank
smell, i with my obdurate
balance outside the act

PART OF A LETTER

i hope you're well, not hungry, not more lonely
than you can bear. i hope you're not angry with me.
i think of you constantly.
                        time goes out, our time
                        goes out for a good time
                        and we're left behind
                        just the same
forgive me for fucking around
forgive me for getting abstract again
                        argument
                        is my meat
                        i wasn't ever cut out
                        for an earth mother. gut talk,
                        yes, but i like games too,
                        make this world as i go along,
                        enjoy the foreplay.
i enjoy you.
i don't want to change you.
if i could be like you
i'd hurt more than i do

have more to tell you
but not the same things.
please enjoy me too.

i hope you find yourself some gentle, gone chessplayer
hard-headed, soft spoken,
knows how to bug you, how to leave you alone,
how to answer you, dig in and not budge,
what to do with his head, what to do with his cock,
when to make you shut up

with so much love

for Carol Bergé

SAY FRIEND

were it the better way
to give you what i know you prize
drown myself in your will, erase
my mind, my individual taste,
all that i am break for your eyes
voice, honesty, submerge, give place
to what you love and i half hate
though i gave all my self away
what should you find to take

oh were it now the heart of wit
and not mere prudence or a dream
to turn and offer what i am,
love still, although you're bound to hate,
trust all to your practiced grace
that you will not turn away from it
but bend and leave your accustomed ways
to love me for love's sake

for Erik and Eve Smit

MAURITS ESCHER'S IMPOSSIBLE /
BUILDINGS

are like mine, his stair
    going up, joins itself, no
        spiral but the same closed
square. his men climb up and up and
    over the same measured
        course. if there is where they haven't
been, they never get there.

            when to go back in space or
            time is to go up or
            down as the artist's mind will
            require of you, to what end serve
            orders and made conventions, our
            disappearing line, our vanishing
            point, our signals, renaissance, globes,
            perspectives. i shift them around, the bare
            numbers, denied ornament or
            setting here.

let a be 1, then a is
whole, he wants to multiply
each quantity he meets but
quits them without change.
let a be 2, see
exploding universe the midas
    touch sprouts, bursts / hairy ass's ears from his troubled
crown, he's doubled into / game for you.
    let a be
a, let 1 be 2. why so i do
constantly, the simple child's
words, the old word
games, the same blunt rhymes.

the construction is
the information. like Escher's it has less
to do with conservation than with
recirculation: to pass the same new
world through me again (let
labored be worked / over)
                        reclaim it
again. if you don't care for
mathematics and science / fiction you won't want
these. the satisfactions are
minimal
        equal
               true
                    austere
                        a discipline
choose
        one.

NOVA

1

my friends are cursing each other, they've packed themselves into
                                    soundtrucks, all night
they shoot greek fire through deep heaven's streets, they ride
                in uniform, bald medallioned suns / ride
green comets, the tails of their anger, they trail long beards,
                                        ill-omened hair
of their outrage over the night of my dreams, all night i hear
        Great Beauty, you are a whore
        Great Beauty, my love, country of passion's play in whom i
            wallow in glory you are a whore.

my friends run to blast each other, their words are dynamite, they break
open my skull's precincts, fair structures, they bring down every
                                        beveled edge
splintered in ruin, make wounds in each other / in all hearts
that house my city, leveled abstraction will be left
when they have left me: not Thou nor I, but *executives / housewives:*

142

generals. their words are napalm, they burn idiosyncrasies of smile,
accent and twiddle and curlicue, down to the bare speech, the common
bone.
i see streets and clotted intersections that held us, that we held in our
minds' maps bubble away down
to rubble, i smell the nerves, the cluttered synapses of my friends'
homes
in me seethe, the sky tastes of barbed wire, i touch the dotted lines
we strung
between star and star of our love's charts; they blink out, dot on
dot / line on line
Great Beauty, you are a pride of crimes, a pride of lines drawn,
a rhythm of lines sung, a rhythm of wrinkles, a rag
Great Beauty, Republic of Intellect in whom i triumph, rag
of accusation, ruin,
animator of ruins, an old crone.

2

i hear the voice i love loud in every speaker, crackling with static,
the big bang
of choice in us crosses my streets, crosses, crosses my mind, signs
my mind of streets,
crosses my voice, my voice of streets, hoarse, turns against me, turns it
against me news / news
my voice   /   is no longer mine.
bright star, nova, no longer mine, blazing into cannibal life,
nova, nova, news i bring in my loud cars, my friends crackle and flame
in my liquid streets,
my mind's heavens, my fields of light, incendiaries of themselves, they
sizzle out: *they* / *they*
they have betrayed us, *they* have ignited us, *they* have made us rockets
/ live bombs.

what constellation remembers there is no *they*
what universe, what nebula where no mind sparks knows now
how *they* have burned out, they lie fallen in ashes, in grey rain,
       in pits where once dead / medalled suns
in a spasm of energy sucked whole galaxies into themselves
compacted, impacted, a universe stamped
       down / to one dense coin.

  it will not be any better when we sleep
  it will not be any better when we sleep

3

Great Beauty, come out of your thunder, break up your charged cars
of fire, let me make you a waste where no car moves / no heat comes.
Great Beauty, burst open your night, break apart each seamed black
nebula, let me make you a furnace where eyes will melt /
          where eyes will melt
to coin, to small suns, to compacted suns we wear on our souls like
          white jewels / hard
jewels, and our lips go cracked all day.

i will take you with me into the mind that kills, the mind that makes
an art of destruction, the mind that is no stranger
Great Beauty, in whom every soul leaps up a hero
Great Beauty, in whom every life scatters at random, barbed
particles of loveliness under heaven's chains of will and splintered stars
Great Beauty, you are not the enemy, you are not out there
Heart of Loveliness, you are not worth the life we waste
we are the force we dread.